At
My Father's Feet

By

Lita P. Ward

At
My Father's Feet

By

Lita P. Ward

Printed in the United States of America

Cover Design: BVS Images & Designs
Editor: So It Is Written, LLC
www.soitiswritten.net

First Printing, 2016
ISBN-13: 978-0692634486
ISBN-10: 0692634487

Dedication

I thank God for allowing me again to pen and produce a project ordained by Him. To my husband, Victor J. Ward, and my family, thank you for your patience, support and love.

To Bishop Claudie H. Wilkins and his beautiful wife, Missionary Deloris Wilkins, thank you for the opportunity and permission to compile just a few words of what I have heard over the past twenty plus years. It has been and continues to be an honor to serve God's anointed servants in the Kingdom of God. May our God continue to crown your heads with His wisdom, grace and favor.

Preface

Luke 10:39-42 (NKJV): *And she had a sister called Mary, who also sat at Jesus' feet and heard His word. But Martha was distracted with much serving, and she approached Him and said, "Lord, do You not care that my sister has left me to serve alone? Therefore tell her to help me." And Jesus answered and said to her, "Martha, Martha, you are worried and troubled about many things. But one thing is needed, and Mary has chosen that good part, which will not be taken away from her."*

I have been blessed to sit under the leadership, teaching and mentoring of the honorable Bishop Claudie H. Wilkins for more than twenty years. It is an honor to be the vessel who compiles just some of the words of wisdom he has imparted into God's flock through sermons and Bible study messages.

Whether it was a Tuesday night Bible study, Sunday morning worship service or an assignment at another church, Bishop Wilkins always moved under the unction of the Holy Spirit and allowed God to have His way.

Some of these penned words will be sweet and some bitter; but all of them will be truth and words to live by. Jesus said, *"The words that I speak unto you, they are spirit and they are life"* (John 6:63b).

These quotes are not in any particular order, although I do note when the message was recorded and the message's title. At the end of the book, you will find several inspired prayers Bishop Wilkins has freely shared, which have been a tremendous blessing to our congregation and those fortunate to have received one. At the end of each prayer, there is space for you to record what you will hear God speaking to your spirit. "He that hath an ear, let him hear what the Spirit saith unto the churches; To him that overcometh will I give to eat of the tree of life, which is in the midst of the paradise of God" (Revelation 2:7).

God has truly blessed my bishop with the gifts of the five-fold ministry, and it would be a shame not to share his giftings with the world. As you read these quotes, allow the Holy Spirit to minister to your inner man. Truth is timeless; therefore, what applied aforetime will still apply and be relevant today.

"Never leave home without your **R.I.B.**: **R**estoration, **I**ncrease and **B**lessing."

"God can open a door without a key because He *is* the Key!"

"Real love is learning how to endure."

"Speak the Word of God until it speaks to you."

From the Bishop's Desk

6-7-15

"He chose you for this test. Therefore, you are equipped. So, don't look for anyone else to do it. Keep in mind that this light affliction is but for a moment. It is working for a far more exceeding weight of glory in your life!"

From the Bishop's Desk
6-16-15

"Everyone should have a time of spiritual growth and maturity. When God wanted His people to move, He allowed persecution to push them out. That is how the process works. He takes the things we are weak to, the things we do not like and the things we are uncomfortable with to develop us."

"Listen not only for what a person is saying, but also for what they are *not* saying."

Do You Serve The Lord?
(Part I)

11-19-12

"Why focus on the hurt when you can focus on the healing?"

God Saved the Best
for Last

11-7-10

"What you hang around is what you will become. Be careful who you spend time with."

"You cannot serve the world and serve God, too. You must serve God with your all."

"A '*Selah Moment*' is when God does something so special that you have to stop and say, "Now, what do you think about that? Look and see what the Lord has done for me!"

Do You Serve The Lord?
(Part II)

11-19-12

"You cannot give God a mixture when you serve Him. I'd rather be gold than brass because gold has been tried, and brass does not last."

God is Doing a Shifting

9-6-11

"Situations are just ways for God to get the glory out of your life."

"If you neglect your home, (i.e., your spouse), someone else will take care of it."

"Where does God fit in your personal mission? If He doesn't fit, then you are pursuing the wrong goals."

The Danger of Too Many Pursuits (Part I)

11-28-10

"God didn't leave you; you left Him. But mercy and repentance brought you back."

"Only God can make up our mess ups."

The Danger of Too Many Pursuits (Part II)

11-28-10

"Faith is not a feeling. It's an act, believing that no matter where I am, God is able to get to me. And when He gets to me, He is able to help me."

"Seek God for as long as it takes to get an answer. Don't let time play with your mind."

"Bury yourself so far in God that you no longer hear yourself."

Manifesting the Power of the Lord's Presence

5-2-10

Obedience + Belief =

Blessings!

From the Bishop's Desk

7-28-13

"The fact that I am connected to God is enough to keep me excited about Him."

"Stand strong behind what you speak. Stay with it until you see the manifestation."

"It's not how you end up, but Who you end up with."

"Don't let what you are going through poison your plans or dreams."

Breaking Out of the Box of Negativity
8-5-12

"You can't change a life, but you can be the light or the instrument to help bring about change."

"It is not about you! It's about the assignment God has given you."

"A touch only deals with a feeling. Impartation deals with a lifetime of blessings. You can forget a touch, but you will never forget impartation."

I Win!
10-7-12

"When God *commands* a blessing, no devil can stop you from getting it."

"Every struggle or purpose has a due date. It will manifest something out of your life that is worthwhile."

"Because you have potential, the devil cannot hold you down or lock you into a place of complacency."

It's My Time and My Turn!
8-12-12

"You are not a victim; you are just forgetful (to what God has already done)".

"Stop looking at the package to determine the goods."

From the Bishop's Desk

4-19-15

"When you don't use your faith, you question God's ability to help you."

What Do You Do When You Are About To Lose Your Miracle?

4-5-15

"It's a love thing when it comes to God. It's not about our gifts and talents."

"The anointing is caught, not bought!"

Getting Rid of an Achan Heart
6-21-15

"In every season, there is a purpose which God has designed for you."

"Your season will not break you, but it will take you to your breakthrough! Your breaking is really for your breakthrough!"

Paul's Eight-Point Stress Reduction Plan

6-19-12

Paul's Eight-Point Stress Reduction Plan
(Phil. 4:4-8)

1. Daily Joy
2. Daily Patience
3. Daily Trust
4. Daily Prayer
5. Daily Reflection
6. Daily Inventory of Good Things
7. Daily Meditation
8. Daily Applications of the Word of God

"The more truth I put in my spirit [reading God's Word], the more truth will come out of my mouth."

Getting Rid of a Lying Spirit

n.d.

"The Holy Spirit does not condemn; He convicts. The devil is the one who condemns and lies to us."

"Every rose comes with thorns. Therefore, you cannot get the beauty without the pain."

How Can We Make a Proper Conclusion About Any Condition?
10-21-12

"For every situation, there is a solution. But, it is your job to approach it through the eyes of faith, not fear."

"Be careful what you release from your mouth."

"Everything you are going through has not escaped God. It is in God. He is in control of it all."

These Are They
11-6-11

"The best way to deal with God is to be real with Him. Tell God the truth about yourself. He already knows anyway."

"Stop hiding behind your title and put up a pleasing life before God."

Getting a Better Picture & Closeness to God Through Intimacy
8-14-12

"Every Scripture will manifest itself in time. Time and seasons bring revelation and understanding of the Scripture."

"It is what it is, and I am who I am, according to the Word."

"Even in your desert place, God is a well of living water. He's ready to spring up and flourish you."

The Latter Rain
9-13-11

"Committing your life to God makes Him real in your life."

"The greatest gift you can give to people is love."

"When you do the will of God and bless others, no blessing will He withhold from you."

"Oh That Men Would Praise God!"
12-25-11

"When you have matters of the heart, you need God's guidance on how to handle them."

"Keep your temple clean so the Lord can dwell within you continually."

"The Word of God does not trick you. But the doctrine of men and the flesh will trick and confuse you, and put you in bondage."

The Importance of the Bible in Our Lives
8-23-11

"If you don't believe it, you will never see it come to pass."

"'Ask, seek and knock" only gets you in the doorway. You must continue to seek God and not doubt in order to receive the manifestation."

"When God delays the answer or the blessing, rest assured that it is working out for your good. All things are working for your good when you are connected to God and in relationship with Him."

Believe to See the Goodness of the Lord

2-12-12

"Get your heart and attitude right to experience the joy of the Lord."
Psalm 51:10-12

"Memorize Psalm 1. It is a major key to experiencing the blessings of God."

"F.A.V.O.R. – Favor Activates Victories On Release!"

"F.A.V.O.R. – Faith Accomplishing Victoriously On Release!"

"Faith will move your mountain, but Favor causes others to move your mountain for you!"

***Let God Surround You
With Favor***

12-31-11

"God is not subject to your trial. But, He does control when it is time for you to come out."

"There will be times when you will have to travail in pain and push for the blessing!"

"If you are going to walk with God, learn His characteristics so you won't give up in the walk. If you are going to walk with God, you have to duplicate who God is."

The Time is Now!
9-18-12

"When you didn't want to come out, or didn't even feel like coming out, God had to drag you out. So just thank God for the drag!"

From the Bishop's Desk

12-7-14

"When you come into your dry season, you will use the anointing to help someone else. Then, that person will use their natural means to help you."
Prophet Elijah, The Widow and Her Son

From the Bishop's Desk

12-16-14

"Unless you suffer defeat, you will never know the taste of victory. Nor will you see it."

What to Do When Trouble Keeps Coming
12-14-12

"Rejoice because this is not the end for you! God has prepared a future just for you."

"If you have arrived at a trial, God has already gone before you and fixed it. You will be able to make it through. The way has already been made."

"Your future consists of events, times and situations. Make sure God is at the center of it all."

Our Future
9-2-12

"Ephesians 1:3b ...*who, has blessed us with all spiritual blessings...*
God has already done it!"

"Jesus helps us see God (the Giver) before we can see the blessing (the gift)."

Blessings, Blessings and More Blessings
6-6-10

"The remedy for guilt is the joy of the Lord. You have the power to release yourself from your own prison."

"God does not hold anything against us because He forgives. We condemn ourselves."

"Without touching one another, there is no feeling. It is the same with God. But when you touch Him, things happen!"

Hope and a Plan
7-13-10

"When God places you in a situation, He has something He wants to bring out of your life and something He wants to put in. It's called *process*."

"Before God can bring anything out of your life, you must first become substance that God can use. It is out of the substance that He creates what He desires you to be."

The Power of Confidence
6-28-98

"Ask God to give you a spiritual ear to hear the revelation of His Word so that you can grow spiritually."

"One must win the battle over the flesh. For the greatest battle one has is within one's self."

Examine Yourself
5-27-99

"The Word of God cannot be overturned or defeated. You can always rely on it."

"The church does not need gifted people. It needs servants with a gift (spiritual)."

"A leader does the things which he asks his followers to do. A dictator does the opposite."

The Imperishable Word of God

9-20-11

"Consult God in everything that you do. You need His direction and guidance."

"Faith always stretches out into the blind."

"God is the type of God that if you touch Him, He will touch you back."

How to Make a Fresh Start

1-1-12

"The more you quote Scripture, the more it will become power for you to live by."

Walking With God In These Last Days

2-21-12

"Interfering in God's purpose for your life or anyone else's will bring stress and worry upon you."

Make the Choice to Do Better

4-3-11

"Be determined to make your today greater than your yesterday!"

"Things will never change until you decide you want change."

"Run your race and finish it, according to your God-given pace. It's not about *when* you finish, just as long as you *do* finish."

You Must Overcome
3-3-13

"God doesn't need a middleman to do His bidding when it comes to the covenant He made with you."

"God's love is not based on how much you love Him. It's based on how much He loves you."

"If you do not worship God in private, you cannot authentically worship Him in a corporate setting."

Loving God Through Worship
3-19-13

"Between your destiny and God, there is a midwife. She can kill it before it is born, or she can allow it to come forth."

"It's time to stand in between the devil and your child and tell him that he will not steal, kill or destroy what God has placed in them!"

The Hebrew Midwives
(Mother's Day Message)

5-12-13

"There are no more players, but now there are vision thieves. So stay focused and on course."

"To make it through these experiences, you need perseverance, persistence and perspective."

What to Do When the Experiences of Life
Leave You Empty

6-2-13

"God wants more Kingdom-minded folks than religious folks."

"Progressive Discipline: When you allow your past to hold you back, thinking that God is punishing you for sins that He has already forgiven and forgotten."

Because of Him

3-31-13

"Faith cometh by hearing. But, what good is it to hear from God if you are not *listening*?"

"You have to *want* to hear what God is saying."

"The Lord's guidance will always contradict the world's philosophy."

Is That You, Lord?

2013

"The people of God would be much better off if they would use God's set of standards instead of their own."

"Follow God's pattern and there will be fewer issues in the church."

Making Sure You Have Clarity

2013

"People who don't value you will always take advantage of you."

"The devourer does not want *you*. He wants what God has placed on the inside of you."

"God does not make us do anything. But, He will show us our wrongdoings."

Watch the Devourer

3-17-13

"Don't even ask God for spiritual gifts if you are not willing to go through the wilderness or testing period."

You Have to Give Up to Go Up

5-5-13

"If you can make an excuse, why can't you make a solution?"

"When you get past the fleece stage, you know that all things are working for your good."

"There are three phases that God takes us through in our spiritual walk: milk, meat and mystery. In the mystery phase, you may not be able to figure out what God is doing, but you won't move from it because you know He is working it out for you!"

Stop Victimizing Your Life

2013

"The Holy Spirt does not work outside of God's Word. So make sure He can find the Word in you."

"The most important thing you should be concerned about is completing your assignment, which is to advance the Kingdom."

Building on the Foundation of Jesus
7-30-13

"God uses real-life situations to mature us and deepen our knowledge of His ways."

"Stop denying God's power by seeking your flesh to solve problems."

"You have to live by what you know about God and not by what you see."

The Knowledge of God
6-11-13

"Knowing God is the secret to success."

"The only season of lack you should experience is the one in which God is testing you."

"It is better to have more power in God than to be powerful in the world."

"Our prayer cry should be, "Lord, I need to reconnect with the Holy Spirit.""

The Knowledge of God (continued)
6-11-13

"When God puts you into a changed (new) environment, you have to become a changed person."

"Most of the devil's power is in your past."

The World, The Devil and The Flesh
5-28-13

"How can you be the light of the world without anything to show for it?"

"After a while, you don't care about a title. You just want the manifestation of the Word in your life."

"Some things, God won't do for us because it's what's best for us."

A Level of Expectation
8-27-13

"You can't pray for people, and then question your own faith."

"Jesus showed the disciples three key marks of his leadership: competence, comprehension and compassion."

Marks of Leadership
In Jesus

10-22-13

"Trust does not have a time limit."

"If you are going to trust God, you must trust Him with all of you, not just part of you."

Trusting God to Keep His Word

2013

"You cannot change the plan of God just because you don't like the process."

"When you rush ahead of God's will, you lose great opportunities to learn more about Him and yourself."

"There is no test that God won't see you through."

Stop Trying to Shortcut God's Will

9-15-13

"Run hard after God. You won't be disappointed."

"What I hear, I think. What I think, I feel. What I feel, I do. And what I do becomes my habits. And my habits determine my destiny."

"Seeking God early means making Him first priority before I make a move."

Change Your Level of Commitment
12-15-13

"When you settle, you never get what God promised you."

"When you grieve the Holy Ghost, you grieve God."

"God won't use or bless a counterfeit."

Don't Settle with the Devil
2013

"Every test isn't easy, but we are assured of the victory."

"A lot of blessings have been aborted because we quit in the middle of labor."

"Eternal eyesight is looking beyond what you actually see."

Communicate to Stay Connected

2013

"When you are helpless, all you need is *some* hope to be hopeful."

"The greater the anointing, the greater attacks and mind battles a person will experience."

"If you have a lively hope, all things that seem impossible can become possible."

Have You Forgotten Hope?

7-4-10

"When you don't do what God says, you have a greater expense to pay."

"It will always cost you more to get the benefit you desire. No one can fill that void, but God."

Paying Recognition to The Word of God
4-18-10

"Three of the scariest words in the English language: surrender to God."

"If you stop trying to be *the god* over your life, then *God* can get the glory out of your life."

What Happens When You Let God Be God in Your Life?
5-16-10

"One must skillfully plan for the attack of the enemy."

"When you pray, use the authority God has given you."

"There will be times when you will have to strive in the spirit to get results."

Warfare Strategies
9-4-12

"There is something in the struggle that is necessary to help you become what God wants you to be."

"God will allow 'giants' in your land to teach you how to walk the walk and talk the talk."

"The church can only reveal God to you. It can't give you a relationship with Him."

Don't Bail Out and Don't Back Down! There is Something Good in the Struggle!
n.d.

"In your struggle, God empowers you. That's why when you come out, the Apostle Paul said, "You are more than a conqueror!'"

"Your destiny is connected to your struggle. Don't forfeit your destiny because you don't want to go through the struggle."

"It's your struggle that is going to bring you power and prosperity."

Don't Bail Out and Don't Back Down! There is Something Good in the Struggle!

n.d.

"Don't let your circumstances dictate your mood."

"Remove all hindrances so that the Holy Spirit can have a continuous flow in your life."

**Changing
and
Charging the Atmosphere**

2010

"Life is unpredictable, unless you know God."

"When dealing with people, look for the good in them instead of the bad."

"One has to be different from the world to make a difference in the world."

Differences That Make a Difference
8-1-10

"God sees something in you worth saving."

"We don't fall because of what comes into our lives. We fall when we yield to it and don't know how to break away from it."

You Need to Try Him for Yourself
1-15-06

"Why not give and simply expect nothing in return? God is the Rewarder."

"The more you empty your heart out to God, the more you can become who God wants you to be."

"Why pretend to be something, when you can be it *for real?*"

It's Time to Give
12-31-13

"You better deliver yourself from people. They will provoke you to miss your blessing."

"When you are not in the order of God, that simply means you're out of order."

Don't Turn Aside
2014

"When you get close to your breakthrough or blessing, the devil will show up to take one last stand against you."

"Pain and confusion are the results of trusting a false promise."

"If you are experiencing pain and confusion in a relationship, deception is somewhere around."

The Spirit of Deception
3-30-14

"The key to getting is sowing."

"Become a bigger thinker, and trust God for more."

"Whatever you feed your mind, that is what you become."

"There are four interlocking dimensions of being:
1)   Body – physical
2)   Mind – thoughts
3)   Emotions – feelings
4)   Spirit – sum total of ourselves"

How to Prosper
3-16-14

"Only God can take nothing and make something out of it."

"You can have power today if you have vision for tomorrow."

"Your vision has to take you farther than you got lifetime to live."

The Pressure Is On! Can You Endure the Race?
6-9-06

"Your praise must be greater than your words!"

"When you refuse to hear God, you refuse to mature."

"Your praise has to be able to go on, even when your flesh doesn't understand why you are doing it."

Your Praise
2-19-05

"When you partake, it means that you are on the Lord's side."

"Partaking means I allow God to become a part of everything about me."

"It is a time of fellowship with the Lord. I am willing to participate in His service just because He is God."

Taking a Serious Look at Communion
2-19-05

"When God gives you another chance, don't take it lightly. Somebody didn't get one!"

"The mess you go through is what creates your growth."

"And when you fall, get up! But don't bring the failure with you when you get up."

I Made It!
1-1-06

"Don't carry so much weight that you are unable to help someone else."

"If you don't talk to your flesh, your flesh will talk to you and take over."

"If a person is not committed to God, he or she cannot and will not be committed to you."

The Pressure is Still On

4-2-06

"You may not know what God is doing, but you do know that He is working out something for your good."

"The devil cannot take your life because you belong to God. He has something working on the inside of you."

"You may not understand what is going on, but something is happening. God has it all worked out."

God's Got a Little Something Working On the Inside

1-13-06

"When you come through the storm, you are going to get off. Get off in praise! Get off with a new focus! Get off with a stronger foundation."

"It's not good enough to just trust God on the side you are on (seen). You have to trust God for what is on the other side (unseen)."

"The storm will reveal whose side you really are on: God's or the devil's."

Lord, Help Me to Go Over to the Other Side
6-28-06

"When God spares your life or brings you out, you are considered to be the redeemed."

"Spirits torment us, not people. Stop fighting people and target the spirits working inside of them."

You're Targeted for a Hit, but God's Got Your Back
6-18-06

"It is a tragic thing when you misplace God. In doing so, you misplace your blessing."

"To get what He has promised you, you must keep God in the right place."

"The quality of your preparation determines the quality of your performance."

The Power of Proper Priorities
2-21-05

"It is your purpose that is under attack, not you."

"Things come, not to take you out of purpose, but to reveal that you *do* have purpose."

"Thank God daily for purpose. When you have purpose, you have life."

"Seek purpose and God will take care of the rest for you; your life is hid in Christ." [Matt. 6:33]

"Job had fear and respect for God, but didn't have perfect love. Yet, after his trials, Job earned it and more." [1 John 4:18... *Perfect love cast out all fear.*]

From the Bishop's Desk
9-22-15

"The Three-Fold Revelation of Jesus Christ is:
1.   He is the Way.
2.   He is the Truth.
3.   He is the Life."

"The three greatest things in your life is:
1.   Your seed
2.   The Holy Spirit
3.   Your assignment"

From the Bishop's Desk
9-22-15

"Righteousness is in a class all by itself."

"Make sure when you ask God for something great, you are willing to pay the price."

"You cannot change or negotiate the steps that God has ordered for you."

Let's Do It Again
(Part I)

12-6-15

"In your dilemma, somebody besides you will get delivered. God never uses your life for a single trial."

"Stop being sure with only being on the shore. It's time to step out into the deep!"

"The best spiritual warfare tactic is to send your praise first."

Let's Do It Again
(Part II)
12-20-15

"Every day is an opportunity to see the blessings of the Lord."

"God will step out of time, in time, just to deliver us."

"You've got to give it up in order to go up!"

Leave the Old Life Behind
5-28-06

"If you praise God in His presence, He will bring power into your situation."

"One act of wrongdoing comes from a root. So if you don't destroy the root, the wrongdoing will continue."

"The greatest person you can become is the person that delivers or helps the person that hurt you."

I Have to Keep Moving! He's Preparing Me for Greater!

12-31-15

"In your weakest moment, God will put more pressure on you to show you that you are not at the end of your potential."

Stand Firm, Be Faithful & Plan to Succeed

8-8-10

"When God straightens things out for us, it always works out for our best interest."

"When you pray according to the Word of God and His will, you will receive the result and return on the investment He promised."

Things that Prevent the Opening of Heaven in Your Life

2-4-03

"Where the Spirit of the Lord is, there is liberty, not legalism."

"When you learn where you have been, you will be blessed in where you are going."

You're Down and Out Because of the Facts & You're Destroyed By Reason of Lack

7-20-03

"Learn to do what it takes to get where you need to be."

"Administer more love in your relationships, and stop playing The Blame Game."

God Wants Your Love, Not Your Offering
9-2-01

"It is never a matter of who is right. It's a matter of doing the right thing."

"Stop entering the house of the Lord dressed up and leaving still messed up."

Tell the Devil to Leave and Then Get Your Healing
9-20-02

"It is better to make a statement out of what we know than what we feel. Feelings can and will deceive us."

"The choices you make determine the blessings of God for your life."

"If you are capable of making a wrong choice, you are also capable of making a right one."

God's Promises
and
Our Choices

12-11-01

"You are not the victim, but the victor!"

"Instead of complaining about who won't help you, help yourself!"

"You can't change what has been, but you can change what happens next."

Get Rid of the
Victim's Mentality
6-1-03

"In our seasons and in time, purpose is revealed."

"When you go through a hard season, an anointing is released on your life for work ordained by God."

God's Got All of This!
6-28-15

"When you are addicted to Jesus, even if you stumble, you won't fall."

"For every trial you go through, there are instructions to go with it."

"The miracle is not that you finished. The miracle is that you started."

I'm Addicted to Jesus and I Will Not Stop!
1-3-16

"Sometimes we just talk too much. We need to get in God's presence, shut up and let Him talk to us."

From the Bishop's Desk
11-8-15

"You are somebody to God, and God is everything to you. Without God, you can go nowhere. But with God, nothing can stop you!"

From the Bishop's Desk
n.d.

"I am not asking God *for* a miracle in 2016; I'm heading *into* 2016 with my miracle!"

New Year's Eve Message

12-31-15

"After you have received your instructions, stay on course by committing to the following acts:
1. Be desperate.
2. Be dissatisfied with the norm.
3. Be devoted.
4. Be determined.
5. Be disciplined."

Get Your Course and Stay On It!
n.d.

"One cannot be complacent with conditions when it comes to following the Lord."

"One cannot be careless with commitment in following the Lord."

The Cost of Discipleship

7-9-07

"We need to serve because...
1. the gift is supplied to you.
2. The gift is given to serve others.
3. the gift is an opportunity and a privilege to be a good steward of God."

Why Do We Need To Serve
7-9-07

"Your testing qualifies you for promotion. Your promotion qualifies you for rewards. Your rewards increase the flow of your joy."

A Time Of Testing
7-16-02

"It is better to save a soul than to save a life."

"God will not come in and mix with the old you. He comes in to make you brand new."

"Before we submit to God, we first have to submit to one another."

"When we walk in submission to others and God, we give concrete evidence that we are filled with the Holy Spirit."

Spirit-Filled Submission

1-12-16

"Truth is a person, while right and wrong are principles of truth."

"Salvation is relational, not informational. It is simply intimacy with God and the Word (Truth)."

Do You Still Believe And Know The Truth?

4-15-12

"G.P.S. – God's Positioning System"

Do You Know Where You Are ?

4-29-12

"Learn the order of God and receive His blessings."

"Stop praying on the run, and make time for God."

Move The Restraints!
5-20-12

"When you do things in your own strength, you will feel a sense of tiredness and weariness. But when it is ordained by God, He will take over for you."

From the Bishop's Desk
7-1-12

"G.R.A.C.E. – God's Riches at Christ's Expense."

"When you go through, God will give you grace."

"Grace helps us to continue on when our prayers go unanswered and things do not change."

"Because of grace, giving up is unjustifiable!"

God's Grace
7-3-12

"Foundational Principles of Love-N-Fellowship Ministries, Inc.
(The 4 P's):
1. The Power of Praise
2. The Perfection of Love
3. The Promise of Fellowship
4. The Proclamation of the Gospel"

From the Bishop's Desk
2005

Prayer For Breakthrough

By Bishop Claudie Wilkins

Lord God, I thank You because You will reward my labor with success and breakthrough. I pray that I just don't see the problems around me, but that I see the breakthrough surrounding me. I give You praise for all the open doors and breakthroughs. Thank You, Lord Jesus for causing me to have victory in You all times. Thank You for declaring me victorious even before the battle. Lord God, manifest Your victory through me.

In the name of Jesus, I take authority over my situation and I command a change! I declare with the help of the Holy Spirit that I will wait until my change comes. I speak to the mountain that I am facing and declare that I will possess my possession. I command every problem that has risen against me to turn around in the name of the Lord Jesus! I command everything that has become a mountain to move in the name of Jesus!

I command that every impossibility begin to transform into the possible! I speak to every fiery situation and declare that it will be transformed to gold in the name of Jesus. I declare before my greatest challenge that I am strong in the name of the Lord Jesus. Lord Jesus, breakthrough is upon my enemies!

I pray for a way in every situation where there seems to be hindrances. I prophesy to every battle that I am facing in the name of Jesus, by the Holy Sprit, and command it to change to a blessing. Lord Jesus, at all times, You will be the Master of my breakthrough!

I declare that every enemy that rises against me shall fall in the name of Jesus. I command every mountain of satanic confrontation to crumble in the name of Jesus. I speak to the mountains of impossibilities and command that they be possible. All my goods, which the enemy has corrupted and destroyed, I command that they be transformed for good in the name of the Lord!

I pray that new blessings and breakthroughs will begin to spring forth for me and mine in the name of Jesus. I pray for the anointing to operate in the creative ideas that are not yet revealed to others.

I confess that the Lord Jesus will cause my change to come. I confess that despite obvious circumstances, I am blessed and highly favoured. I prophesy on the circumstances, seen and unseen, that the Lord will bless me and wipe away the remembrance of failure and setbacks.

I push back every limitation built up around my life and dreams by the enemy in the name of Jesus. I prophesy to every unproductive area in my life for Christ's sake and command it to bring forth fruit. Thank You, God! You will cause new wells to spring up in all my desert places.

God, I praise You because You will bear me up on eagles' wings, even before my enemies! Thank you, Lord God! You will get the glory out of my life. I am blessed and highly favoured! Amen!

NOTES – *(What did I hear God say to me?)*

_____

_____

_____

_____

_____

_____

_____

_____

_____

_____

_____

_____

_____

_____

_____

_____

Prescription for Divine Health

By Bishop Claudie Wilkins

(Proverbs 4:20-24)

Read the following
Confession and Healing
Scriptures daily:

In the Name of Jesus, we command the electrical and chemical frequencies in every cell in our bodies to be in harmony and balance in Jesus' name. Father God, digest any bad cells in our bodies. We also confess that our minds will never grow dull. Our eyes will never grow dim. Our ears will never grow deaf. Our mouths will always speak the Word of God and no cancer, no heart attack, no stroke nor any other debilitating disease will ever come against our bodies!

"I will put none of these diseases upon you...for I am the Lord, who heals you." Exodus 15:26

"And I will take sickness away from the midst of you." Exodus 23:25

*Bless the Lord, O my soul, and forget not all His benefits: Who forgives all your iniquities, Who heals all
your diseases.*
Psalm 103:2-3

He sent His Word and healed them...
Psalm 107:20

But he was wounded for our transgressions, He was bruised for our iniquities: the chastisement of our peace was upon him; and with His stripes we are healed. Isaiah 53:5

"But to you who fear My name, the Sun of Righteousness shall arise with healing in His wings…"
Malachi 4:2

And Jesus went about all Galilee, teaching in their synagogues, and preaching the gospel of the kingdom, and healing all manner of sickness and all manner of disease among the people.
Matthew 4:23

When evening had come, they brought Him any who were demon-possessed. And He cast out the spirits with a Word and healed all who were sick, that it might be fulfilled which was spoken by Isaiah the prophet, saying, "He Himself took our infirmities and bore sickness."'
Matthew 8:16 -17

"My son, give attention to my words; incline your ear to my sayings, for they are life to those who find them and health to all their flesh."
Proverbs 4:20, 22

And the prayer of faith shall save the sick…
James 5:15

*Who Himself bore our sins in His own body on the
tree, that we, having died to sins,
might live for righteousness:
by whose stripes you were healed.*
1Peter 2:24

NOTES – (What did I hear God say to me?)

_____

_____

_____

_____

_____

_____

_____

_____

_____

_____

_____

_____

_____

_____

_____

_____

_____

Prayer for Finances

<u>By Bishop Claudie Wilkins</u>

Abba Father, I believe and confess that You are good and Your faithfulness is ever sure: (EL ELYON = *Most High God*). I pray that You give me a giver's heart so that I may increase according to Your promise.

I pray for debt cancellation and ask for the grace and blessing that will make me a lender and not a borrower. Lord God, I declare by faith that the rest of my years shall not be in a struggle but prosperity: (EL SHADDAI = *God is more than enough*). Lord, let the harvest meet the harvest in my life. Open my eyes that I may see the good ground in ministry to sow my seeds of finance. I pray for the ability to be a Kingdom-promoter, using my finances for the ministry: (JEHOVAH JIREH = *The Lord will provide*). Father, I speak into my future a continuous lifestyle of blessing and favor.

I pray that despite the attack of the enemy, it will all result in promotion and the favor of God. I declare, Father, that because my faith is in You, I will never lack any good thing: (EL SHADDAI = *God is more than enough*). Even in the face of financial setback, I declare that Your plan and covenant of blessings shall stand: (EL ELYON = *Most High God*). Lord

God, I believe and confess that I am already loaded with Your benefits.

I possess a future of abundant wealth for myself and my children in the name of Jesus. Father, I pray for the wisdom to be a wise steward of God's provision. Lord, give me the strength to keep the blessings You are bringing into my life.

I pray that every step I take will result in blessings and increase. I confess that I have my liberty from every form of indebtedness. I thank you, Jehovah God, because Your divine power has provided all my needs for life and godliness.

FOUNDATIONAL SCRIPTURES:

Genesis 26:12   Job 42:12   2Peter 1:3

Isaiah 48:17   3 John 2   Luke 12:34

Romans 13:8   Galatians 6:6-9

Ephesians 3:20   Mark 4:8

Philippians 4:17, 19

Deuteronomy 6:3; 16:17; 32:11

Psalms 23:5-6; 35:27; 66:12; 84:11

Psalms 34:10; 37:25; 68:19; 112:1-3, 5

Proverbs 3:9-19; 11:16; 12:24; 13:4, 22

NOTES – (What did I hear God say to me?)

_____

_____

_____

_____

_____

_____

_____

_____

_____

_____

_____

_____

_____

_____

_____

_____

_____

_____

Prayer of Divine Protection

By Bishop Claudie Wilkins

Personal Confession: "The Lord is my protection; therefore, no evil can harm me."

As mountains surround Jerusalem, so does God's presence surround me and all who dwell with them. Psalm 125:2

The Lord is my Shepherd; His rod and staff shield me from grievous and ravenous forces. Psalm 23

I dwell in a secret place known only to my heavenly Father; therefore Satan cannot find me. Psalm 27:5

In the name of the Lord do I trust, within Him is salvation forever. Proverbs 18:10

Through fire, storm, earthquake, or flood, He is my constant companion covering me with His hand; sheltering me in His shadow. Psalm 57:1
I abide beneath His everlasting arm, where I am safe now and throughout eternity. Deuteronomy 33:27

The strength of my life is He; neither foe nor wicked enemy can devour my flesh. Psalm 27:1-2

My heart shall not be cast down to despair over departed joys of yesterday. God is my hope for new and greater joys on tomorrow.
Psalm 42:11

The Lord preserveth my life as I come in, as I go out and even as I slumber and sleep.
Psalm 121:7-8

There is no more fear in me because through love and faith, I have complete confidence in Jesus Christ.
1 John 4:18

CONFESSION: This is my affirmation of prayer and protection for myself, all who dwell with me and all who are dear to me.

_____
Your Signature of Faith

I have prayed for thee,
That thy faith fail not...
Luke 22:32

NOTES – (What did I hear God say to me?)

_____

_____

_____

_____

_____

_____

_____

_____

_____

_____

_____

_____

_____

_____

_____

_____

_____

Prayer Points to Pray When Your Heavens Become Brass

By Bishop Claudie Wilkins

1. My heavens, open by fire, in the name of Jesus.
2. You, my enemies, shall not prevail, in the name of Jesus.
3. O God, arise in my life and let the world know that you are my God, in the name of Jesus.
4. My hidden riches, be revealed and be released, in the name of Jesus.
5. O windows of Heaven, open unto my life, in the name of Jesus.
6. Satanic brass of iron that is working against me, shatter, in the name of Jesus!
7. Sun, moon and stars, refuse to cooperate with my enemies, in the name of Jesus.
8. Every power that has been assigned to sit on my breakthrough, die, in the name of Jesus!

NOTES – (What did I hear God say to me?)

_____

_____

_____

_____

_____

_____

_____

_____

_____

_____

_____

_____

_____

_____

_____

_____

_____

_____

Meet the Bishop

Bishop Claudie H. Wilkins began fulfilling his call to the ministry in 1982 and began his training in the doctrine of the Church of God in Christ in the state of New Jersey. In 1984, he was licensed as an associate minister of Bible Way COGIC in Orange, New Jersey and two years later, ordained as an elder. In 1989, Bishop Wilkins heard the greater call from God for the pastorate to move to Williamston, North Carolina, where Little Thankful Holy Church was founded, right in the living room of his aunt, the late Mother Naomi Griffin. In 2004, Bishop Wilkins was consecrated to the office of Bishop in the International Council of Pentecostal Ministries by the Presiding Prelate of ICOPM, the honorable Bishop William S. Spain.

In 2005, God blessed him to become the Presiding Prelate of Love-N-Fellowship Ministries, Inc., an interdependent, interdenominational, international fellowship of churches and ministries dedicated to perfecting the church and affecting the communities we serve. Finally, in 2015, Little Thankful Holy Church became Little Thankful Praise and Presence Ministry, with one location in Williamston, North Carolina and the second one in Jacksonville, North Carolina.

His most recent achievement occurred on November 3, 2015 when he was elected as Robersonville, North Carolina's Town Commissioner, Council At-large. He has always been concerned and active in the community, showing his love for people and striving to make a difference. Bishop Wilkins has been married 43 years to his lovely wife, Missionary Deloris Wilkins and they are the proud parents of five children, twelve grandchildren and two great grandchildren.

For more information or to contact Bishop, please call 252-809-0151 or email him at cdwlthc@suddenlink.net.

Meet the Author

Lita P. Ward is an ordained evangelist and author. She is also the CEO and owner of LPW Editing Services, which provides professional editing and proofreading for authors, students, businesses and job seekers. There is no job too small or large for her company. Their motto is *Inspired by Vision; Driven by Purpose.* LPW Editing Services ensures that once a client's project leaves their hands, the product is polished and professional.

Also, Evangelist Ward diligently and faithfully has served at Little Thankful Praise and Presence Ministry under the great leadership of Bishop Claudie H. Wilkins for over twenty years as a missionary, Sunday school teacher, youth director, and clerk. In 2008, she accepted her call into the ministry and was ordained and licensed by Bishop Claudie H. Wilkins as a minister at Little Thankful Holy Church and Love-N-Fellowship Ministries. In 2009, the Lord assigned to her humble hands a women's ministry entitled L.T.H.C. DOVES (Divinely Ordained as Vessels to Encourage, Equip and Empower). Her desire is to please the Lord and walk in her vocation of purpose and destiny. Her focus is servanthood and Kingdom-building as she ministers and teaches the Word of God.

Join Lita on Social Media:

Lita P Ward   *@LitaPWard*

Also, connect with Lita on her multiple Facebook pages to be inspired:

Lita P. Ward

Lita P Ward

LPW Editing Services

To book Lita as a speaker for your next event, please submit your request to lita.ward1@gmail.com. For editing services, please email her at lpwediting@gmail.com.

Website: www.litapward.com

Ordering Information:
Quantity Sales. Special discounts are available on quantity purchases by corporations, associations, and others. For details, contact Lita P. Ward at lita.ward1@gmail.com or www.litapward.com

ALSO BY LITA P. WARD:

The Little Girl With The Want To

www.ingramcontent.com/pod-product-compliance
Lightning Source LLC
Chambersburg PA
CBHW040056100426
42734CB00034B/2